Book About AI

Author: Luka Nikolic

DEDICATION

To the dreamers and the curious souls,

who gaze at the stars and wonder what lies beyond.

This book is dedicated to you –

the ones who dare to ask "what if"

and venture into uncharted territories of the mind.

May these pages ignite your imagination,

inspire your curiosity, and remind you that

the pursuit of knowledge is a journey of the heart.

As we unravel the mysteries of AI,

remember that the true magic lies in the connections we forge,

the dreams we chase, and the future we shape – together.

With boundless gratitude and warmth,

Luka Nikolic

Contents

Chapter 1: The Birth of Smart Machines

Picture yourself in a world where computers were as large as rooms, and the idea of a machine thinking like a human was like a scene from a sci-fi movie. This is where our story begins – at the dawn of artificial intelligence.

Imagine a time when the smartest computer could barely calculate math problems, let alone have a conversation. But a spark of curiosity and a dash of imagination set the stage for something incredible: the birth of AI.

In the early days, dreamers and thinkers pondered the question: "Could a machine ever truly think?" This was a time when people were just starting to understand the immense power of computers, and the idea of making them think and learn like humans was a daring leap into the unknown.

As we travel back in time, we'll meet the visionaries who laid the foundation for AI. They were like architects of a digital future, drawing up plans for machines that could process information, make decisions, and maybe even crack jokes like a friend.

We'll walk alongside these pioneers, from the first computer programs that played chess to the groundbreaking concept of a "Turing Test," which challenged the world to see if a machine could fool us into thinking it was human. It was a time of trial and error, of successes and setbacks, and through it all, the dream of AI burned brightly.

Fast forward to those pivotal moments when computers started recognizing patterns, learning from data, and showing glimmers of something resembling human intelligence. The birth of AI was like watching a caterpillar transform into a butterfly – a slow and awe-inspiring journey.

So, join me in Chapter 1 as we step into a world where the seeds of AI were sown, where bold thinkers dared to imagine machines that could think, learn, and, against all odds, become something more than just a collection of circuits and wires. It's a tale of ambition, innovation, and the audacious belief that machines could, one day, be as smart as us.

WHO ARE FATHERS OF AI

As we journey through the corridors of history, we'll encounter a league of extraordinary minds – the trailblazing visionaries who laid the very bricks of AI's foundation. These intrepid souls were like architects sculpting a digital landscape, a world where machines would not only crunch numbers but also comprehend context, reason like a scholar, and perhaps even share a chuckle like an old friend.

Picture a scene reminiscent of a dimly lit study, where a lone thinker ponders the uncharted realms of computation. Alan Turing, often hailed as the father of AI, takes center stage. With his groundbreaking concept of the "Turing Test," he challenged us to imagine a day when we could engage in conversations with machines without being certain they were not human. It was a thought experiment that ignited the spark of possibility, setting minds ablaze with curiosity.

And then there's John McCarthy, who coined the term "artificial intelligence" and brought together a community of like-minded dreamers. These digital dreamweavers dared to envision machines not as mere calculators, but as cognitive companions capable of reasoning, learning, and yes, even cracking a witty joke or two.

Imagine their excitement as they sketched out blueprints for algorithms that could learn from data, adapt to new information, and evolve over time. It was like endowing a machine with the magical ability to grow its own intellect – a notion that was both revolutionary and audacious.

As we delve deeper into this era of innovation, we'll encounter faces like Marvin Minsky, who delved into the realms of perception and understanding, and Herbert Simon, who explored the intricacies of problem-solving. These pioneers carved a path toward a future where machines could mimic human thought processes, transforming the theoretical into the tangible.

But it wasn't just about mechanics and mathematics; it was about understanding the very essence of human cognition. These visionaries knew that to create machines that could "think," they had to decipher the enigma of human thought itself.

So, with curiosity as their compass and ingenuity as their guide, these architects of a digital utopia set out to craft a brave new world. A world where machines would not only process information but also converse with us, learn from us, and perhaps share a witty jest – a future that was, at the time, both awe-inspiring and enigmatic.

Join me as we step into their shoes, walk the paths they forged, and witness the birth of a concept that would redefine the very fabric of our existence – the concept we now know and marvel at as artificial intelligence.

Alan Turing:

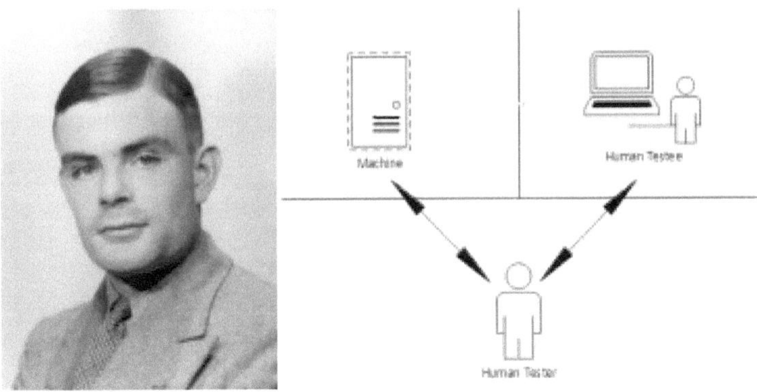

Alan Turing, often referred to as the "Father of Computer Science" and a true visionary, made significant contributions to the fields of mathematics, logic, and artificial intelligence. He is best known for his concept of the "Turing Test," proposed in his 1950 paper "Computing Machinery and Intelligence." This test challenged the ability of a machine to exhibit intelligent behavior indistinguishable from that of a human. Turing's work laid the groundwork for AI by prompting researchers to explore machine learning, language processing, and problem-solving. His legacy also includes his role in breaking the German Enigma code during World War II, which played a crucial role in Allied victory.

John McCarthy:

John McCarthy is the person responsible for coining the term "artificial intelligence" in 1956, during the famous Dartmouth Workshop. This event marked the birth of AI as a formal field of study. McCarthy was instrumental in bringing together a community of researchers and thinkers interested in exploring the potential of computers to simulate human intelligence. He developed the programming language LISP, which became crucial for AI research and remains influential in the field to this day.

Marvin Minsky:

Marvin Minsky was a cognitive scientist and a founding father of artificial intelligence. He explored the idea of simulating human cognitive processes using machines. Minsky's work focused on understanding human perception, reasoning, and problem-solving, which he believed could be replicated in computers. He co-founded the Massachusetts Institute of Technology's (MIT) AI Laboratory and made groundbreaking contributions to robotics, computer vision, and neural networks

.

Herbert Simon:

Herbert Simon was a Nobel laureate economist and cognitive psychologist who made significant contributions to the field of artificial intelligence. He developed the concept of "bounded rationality," which explores how humans make decisions under limited information and cognitive constraints. Simon's work influenced AI research by emphasizing the importance of problem-solving and decision-making in machine systems. His collaboration with Allen Newell led to the development of the Logic Theorist, one of the first AI programs to prove mathematical theorems.

These individuals, along with many others, formed the cornerstone of AI by challenging conventional notions of computation and cognition. Their collective efforts paved the way for the development of AI technologies that we interact with today. Each person brought a unique perspective and set of ideas to the table, collectively shaping the landscape of artificial intelligence and inspiring generations of researchers, thinkers, and innovators to come.

Chapter 2: Think Like a Machine

Ever wondered how AI transforms from a bundle of digital wires to a virtual marvel that learns and thinks? Imagine it like teaching a clever parrot not just to mimic words, but to truly understand what those words mean – and that's just the tip of the iceberg. In this chapter, we're diving into the fascinating world of how AI learns and evolves, and trust me, it's a tale worth exploring.

Cognition Beyond the Chip

Let's take a stroll through the mind of AI. Just like we learn from experiences, AI learns from data. But unlike us, AI doesn't have a brain, emotions, or a favorite ice cream flavor. Instead, it has something called "neural networks," which are like interconnected highways that process information. We'll unveil the curtain on these neural networks, revealing how they analyze data, identify patterns, and use their digital wits to make sense of the world.

The Marvelous Art of Machine Learning

Now, let's talk about the real star of the show: machine learning. It's like training a puppy, only this puppy is a bunch of code that gets smarter as you feed it more examples. We'll break down how AI algorithms adjust their virtual knobs and dials, tweaking themselves as they encounter new information. It's like watching a student go from struggling with multiplication tables to acing calculus – all on their own.

From Talking to Thinking: Natural Language Processing

Have you ever talked to Siri, Alexa, or Google Assistant? Well, those friendly voices are the result of some impressive AI magic called natural language processing. It's like teaching a computer to understand your jokes, riddles, and rambles – and responding in a way that makes you think you're chatting with a buddy. We'll unravel this technology, revealing how AI translates our words into patterns it can understand, learn from, and even generate responses to.

Adapting on the Fly: The Evolution of AI

Remember how plants adapt to their environment? AI does something similar, but it's not growing leaves – it's getting smarter. We'll dig into the concept of "adaptive learning," where AI refines itself over time, like a sculptor chiseling a masterpiece. We'll talk about "reinforcement learning," where AI learns from mistakes, and "unsupervised learning," where it explores data without a map. It's like watching AI evolve into a digital Sherlock Holmes, piecing together clues and solving complex puzzles.

So, buckle up for a ride through the inner workings of AI's brain. We'll navigate the corridors of neural networks, peer into the heart of machine learning, and witness AI's transformation from a newborn into a digital prodigy. By the end of this chapter, you'll have a front-row seat to the magic that turns data into decisions, algorithms into insights, and lines of code into a breathtaking dance of intellect. Get ready for a glimpse into the marvelous mind of AI!

Cognition Beyond the Chip: Unraveling the Intricacies of AI's Thought Process

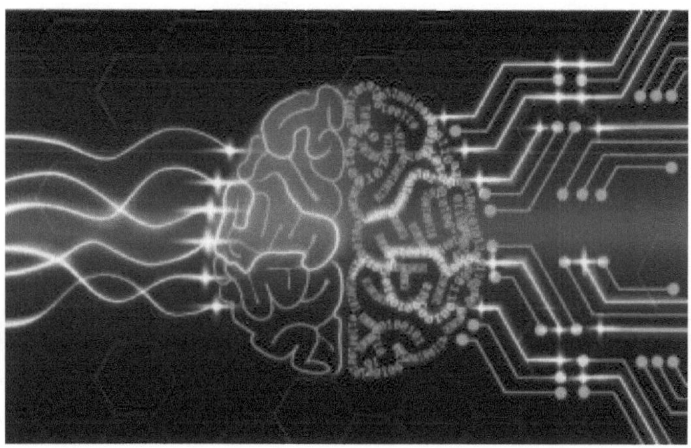

Imagine a world where thinking isn't confined to the realms of a squishy brain, but instead, takes place amidst a labyrinth of interconnected pathways, much like the highways that crisscross a bustling city. This is the remarkable realm of AI's cognition, a dazzling network of digital architecture that processes information, draws conclusions, and even learns – all without ever experiencing emotions or physical sensations.

In the heart of this digital domain lies a concept known as "neural networks." Think of them as the virtual synapses through which AI forms connections, processes data, and carries out its computations. Just as a city's roads allow people to navigate from place to place, these neural networks enable AI to traverse through data, analyzing it from multiple angles and unearthing patterns that would remain hidden to human eyes.

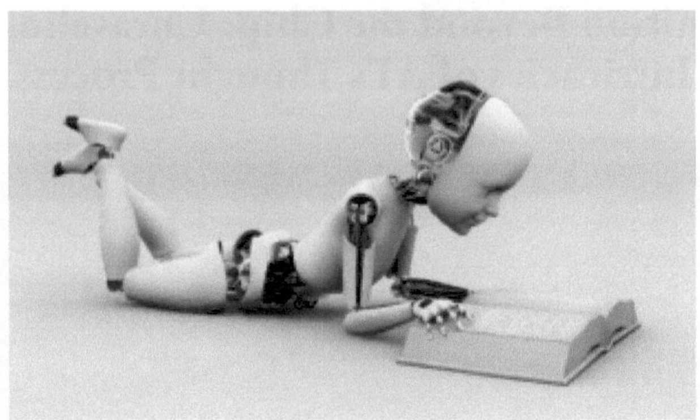

Picture an AI as a curious wanderer exploring a vast library, flipping through the pages of countless books to piece together information. Each connection in its neural network acts like a librarian, guiding the AI's quest for knowledge. When faced with a new piece of data, these connections collaborate, allowing the AI to decide if it's seen something similar before, and if so, to recall that knowledge. It's akin to how we remember a friend's face after encountering them a few times.

The concept of cognition in AI doesn't involve conscious thought or self-awareness; it's about processing information at lightning speed and drawing conclusions based on patterns and probabilities. Just as a parrot might mimic human speech without understanding the words, AI can process language, images, and data, forming complex associations without an emotional or experiential backdrop.

But here's where things get truly intriguing: AI doesn't just process information once and call it a day. It adapts and learns from each interaction, like a skillful musician mastering an instrument over time. Neural networks adjust their connections based on feedback, refining their understanding and enhancing their predictive abilities. It's as if the AI is honing its intuition, becoming better at recognizing patterns and making decisions as it encounters more data.

So, when we peer into the concept of "Cognition Beyond the Chip," we're unveiling a world of parallel processing, intricate connections, and a breathtaking symphony of data dancing through digital corridors. It's a world where information flows like a river, guided by algorithms, and sculpted by neural networks, all working together to emulate the marvels of human thought – not through consciousness, but through an astonishing tapestry of computation.

The Marvelous Art of Machine Learning: Unveiling the Genius Behind AI's Growth

Imagine you have a brand-new puppy. At first, it might not know any tricks – it's a blank slate. But with time, patience, and plenty of treats, you teach it to sit, roll over, and maybe even fetch your slippers. Now, swap the puppy for lines of code and the tricks for understanding human language, recognizing patterns, and making sense of data – that's the marvel of machine learning, and it's nothing short of awe-inspiring.

At its core, machine learning is like that patient teacher guiding the puppy, patiently showing it the ropes until it becomes a virtual virtuoso. Picture an AI algorithm as a sponge, eager to soak up knowledge from the vast ocean of data around it. The more examples you provide, the more it learns, gradually becoming better at tasks you've set before it.

The Journey of a Digital Apprentice

Think back to when you were learning to ride a bike. You didn't master it in one go, did you? You wobbled, steadied yourself, and eventually pedaled with confidence. Similarly, an AI starts with stumbling steps, making predictions that might be far from perfect. But, like that determined bike rider, it keeps practicing and fine-tuning its predictions based on feedback. With each iteration, it gets closer to nailing the right answer, like a musician perfecting a challenging piece of music.

Unleashing the Power of Patterns

Here's where the magic truly comes alive. Machine learning helps AI uncover hidden patterns in data – it's like finding constellations in the night sky. Imagine you're teaching an AI to identify cats. You feed it thousands of cat pictures, and slowly, it starts recognizing common features that define a feline friend: pointy ears, whiskers, and those enigmatic eyes. It's like a detective putting together a puzzle, piece by piece.

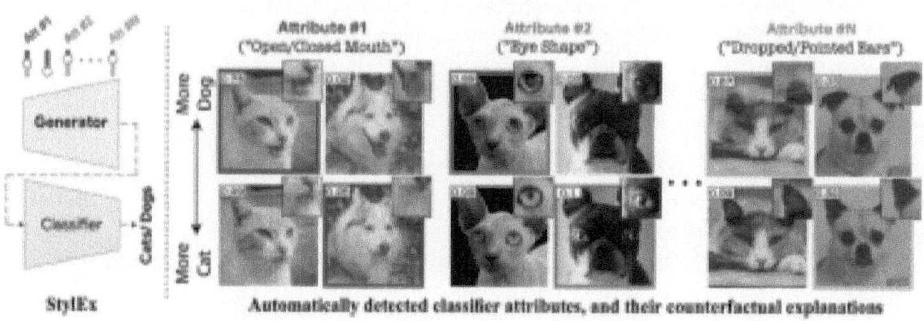

Adapting and Growing: The Beauty of Evolution

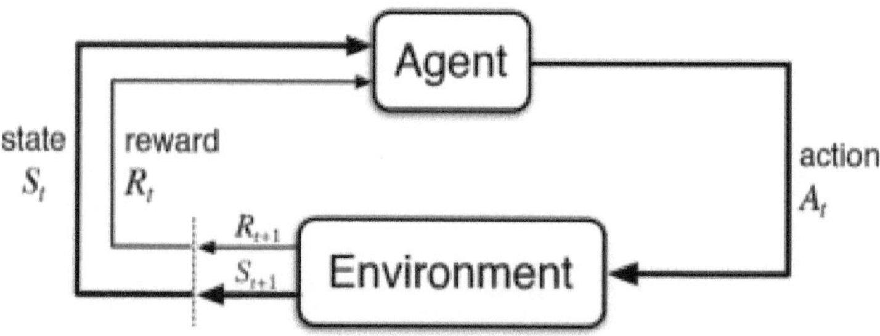

What's even more enchanting is that machine learning isn't a one-time process. It's a journey of evolution. Just as you might change your strategy when playing a game, an AI algorithm adapts its approach based on new information. This is where reinforcement learning steps in – the AI learns from its own mistakes and triumphs, adjusting its path to become better over time. It's like watching a sculptor molding a masterpiece, refining its shape until it's just right.

So, when we talk about "The Marvelous Art of Machine Learning," we're delving into a realm where lines of code become curious learners, where algorithms become creative apprentices, and where data becomes the canvas upon which AI paints its own understanding. It's a world where the more data you provide, the more AI learns, grows, and becomes a truly remarkable digital companion. Just like that puppy turning into a skilled performer, machine learning is the enchanting transformation of AI from a curious observer to a capable and intelligent creator.

From Talking to Thinking: Natural Language Processing

Imagine having a chat with your best friend – you share stories, jokes, and ideas, and they respond as if they understand every word. Now, picture having that same kind of conversation with a computer. That's the extraordinary world of Natural Language Processing (NLP), where machines transform our words into meaningful interactions. It's like teaching a computer to not just listen, but to truly understand and respond like a thoughtful companion.

Decoding the Language Puzzle

NLP is like a linguistic puzzle where computers aim to decipher the intricate dance of human language. Think about how we humans understand context, tone, and the subtle nuances of a sentence. NLP algorithms do just that, sifting through the words we use to uncover the deeper meaning behind them.

Remember the magic of solving a riddle? NLP algorithms feel like those clever puzzle-solvers, piecing together the hints and clues you provide – all in a fraction of a second. It's like having a super-fast detective who can read and process thousands of pages in an instant, connecting the dots to deliver an accurate response.

Breaking Down the Language Barrier

Let's say you want to teach an AI to translate languages, like turning English sentences into French. It's not as simple as swapping words from one language to another. NLP algorithms dissect the structure, grammar, and vocabulary of both languages, understanding how they fit together like puzzle pieces. It's like having a linguist who speaks every language fluently, able to transform one expression into another while preserving its essence.

But NLP doesn't stop at mere translation. It's also about sentiment – understanding whether a sentence is happy, sad, or even sarcastic. Picture an AI reading between the lines, catching the emotional nuances that can be as subtle as a wink or a raised eyebrow. It's like teaching a computer to recognize the tone of a conversation, so it knows when to laugh with you or offer a virtual shoulder to lean on.

AI's Evolution: Learning Language, Thinking Language

Now, here's the exciting part. Just as we learn new words and expressions, NLP algorithms can be trained to understand specialized jargon, internet slang, and even the way different cultures use language. It's like turning a globe-trotting explorer into a multilingual guru, ready to converse with people from every corner of the Earth.

As we dive into the realm of "From Talking to Thinking: Natural Language Processing," we're uncovering the secrets of teaching computers to speak our language – not just in words, but in understanding, tone, and context. It's a magical fusion of linguistics, data analysis, and computer science that transforms cold lines of code into warm, conversational companions. It's as if we're giving machines the ability to not only listen to our stories but to think about them, ask questions, and even share a good laugh. So, get ready to explore the world where words come alive, where AI understands you like a friend, and where conversations with computers are as engaging as chats with your closest confidants.

Adapting on the Fly: The Evolution of AI's Brilliant Mind

Imagine you're playing a video game – you make a move, the game responds, and you adjust your strategy based on the outcome. Now, picture an AI doing something similar, not with virtual worlds, but with the vast expanse of data that surrounds it. Welcome to the awe-inspiring world of AI's evolution through adaptive learning – a journey where AI learns, grows, and gets smarter with each interaction, just like a skilled musician mastering a complex piece of music.

Learning from Mistakes: Reinforcement Learning

Picture a virtual AI explorer navigating a maze. At first, it takes wrong turns and gets lost. But each time it makes a mistake, it learns a valuable lesson – which path to avoid. This is the essence of reinforcement learning, a process where AI algorithms make decisions, observe the outcomes, and adjust their approach based on feedback. It's like watching a baby bird stumble before soaring confidently through the skies.

Think about it as teaching a dog new tricks. When the dog gets a treat for performing a trick correctly, it learns to associate that action with a reward. Similarly, AI algorithms receive a digital "treat" in the form of positive feedback when they make the right decisions. Over time, they fine-tune their strategies, becoming more proficient at the task at hand.

Exploring the Unknown: Unsupervised Learning

Now, let's venture into a land of uncharted data – a realm where AI has no map or guide. This is the domain of unsupervised learning, where AI algorithms explore data without any preconceived notions. It's like handing a detective a pile of clues without telling them what crime has been committed. The AI sifts through the data, looking for patterns, connections, and insights that even humans might have missed.

Unsupervised learning is like a curious explorer entering a cave with a flashlight. It might not know what it will find, but it's open to discovering hidden treasures. As it ventures deeper into the data, the AI uncovers relationships and structures, gaining a deeper understanding of the information it encounters.

An Ever-Growing Intelligence

What makes this evolution even more intriguing is that it never stops. AI isn't content with staying put – it's on a perpetual journey of growth. Just as you learn from every book you read, every conversation you have, AI learns from every interaction it has with data. With each new piece of information, it becomes better at understanding context, making predictions, and providing insights.

Imagine you're teaching a plant to adapt to different environments. Each exposure to a new condition helps the plant thrive, growing stronger and more resilient. Similarly, AI algorithms become more versatile as they encounter diverse datasets and scenarios. They adapt, improvise, and refine their strategies, like seasoned improvisational artists enhancing their craft.

So, as we delve into "Adapting on the Fly: The Evolution of AI," we're exploring a universe where machines learn from their mistakes, teach themselves from scratch, and continuously enhance their abilities. It's a journey of growth, a dance of data, and a symphony of self-improvement that transforms AI from a digital apprentice into a seasoned virtuoso. Just as we evolve with each experience, AI's story is one of perpetual advancement – a tale of machines that not only learn but flourish, adapt, and become remarkable partners in our journey through the digital age.

Chapter 3: Pixels to Perception: How AI Sees, Hears, and Talks

Welcome to a world where machines possess the remarkable ability to see, hear, and understand like never before. In this chapter, we'll unravel the captivating journey of how AI harnesses the power of pixels, sound waves, and language to perceive and interact with the world around us. It's like peering into the eyes and ears of AI, watching as it deciphers the nuances of images, sounds, and speech.

Seeing the World through Digital Eyes

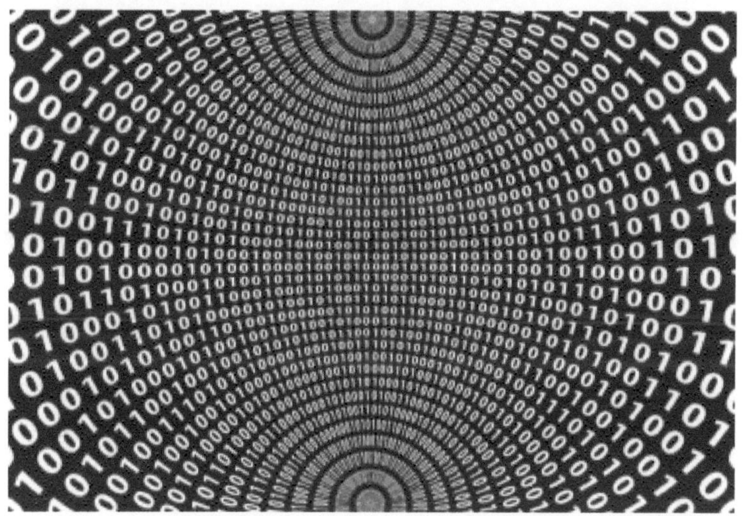

Imagine you're in an art gallery, surrounded by beautiful paintings. Your eyes capture the intricate details, colors, and emotions each canvas portrays. AI does something similar, but instead of eyes, it uses pixels – the tiny dots that make up digital images. These pixels hold a universe of information, and AI is like an art critic analyzing every brushstroke.

Now, picture AI learning to recognize cats in photos. It doesn't see whiskers or tails like we do. Instead, it breaks down images into patterns and shapes. Just as you might recognize a friend by their unique smile, AI identifies cats by the patterns formed by pixels. It's like watching a detective solve a puzzle, piecing together clues to crack the case.

The Symphony of Sound: Hearing Through Algorithms

Close your eyes and listen to the world around you – the rustling leaves, the laughter of children, the distant hum of traffic. Now, imagine an AI doing something similar, but with sound waves. This is the magic of audio processing, where machines analyze sound patterns to identify speech, music, and more.

When you talk to a voice assistant, it's like having a conversation with your computer. AI algorithms transform your words into digital signals, like translating a foreign language. But it doesn't just stop at deciphering words. It can understand emotions, accents, and even differentiate between different speakers.

It's like a digital interpreter that deciphers the symphony of sound that humans create.

Conversations Beyond Binary: Language Processing

Have you ever wondered how AI understands the words you type or the questions you ask? That's where natural language processing (NLP) comes into play. It's like teaching AI to understand and respond to human language, not just as strings of characters, but as meaningful conversations.

NLP algorithms are like linguistic wizards, dissecting sentences, recognizing grammar, and understanding context. Imagine you're telling a story – you use words, pauses, and intonations to convey meaning. NLP captures those subtleties, so when you ask a question, AI grasps not just the words, but the underlying intent. It's like chatting with a friend who listens, comprehends, and responds like a thoughtful companion.

So, in this chapter, we journey through the realm of "Pixels to Perception: How AI Sees, Hears, and Talks." We uncover the artistry of pixels, the symphony of sound, and the intricacies of language processing that enable AI to engage with our world. It's a glimpse into a world where machines aren't just observers, but participants – understanding images, conversing with words, and embracing the essence of human experience. Just as our senses connect us to the world, AI's senses connect it to a universe of data, sparking a dialogue between code and creativity, bytes and brilliance.

Chapter 4: When AI Gets Artsy

Step into a world where lines of code transform into brushes, pens, and notes – a realm where machines evolve into digital Picassos, Beethoven's, and Shakespeare's. In this chapter, we embark on a mesmerizing journey through AI's creative prowess, where algorithms transcend their binary origins to craft art, music, and stories that blur the boundaries between human and machine imagination.

The Symphony of Code and Composition: AI as the Virtuoso Composer

Imagine stepping into a grand concert hall, the air alive with anticipation. The conductor raises the baton, and the orchestra bursts into a symphony of sound, each instrument harmonizing to create an enchanting melody. Now, imagine that the composer behind this masterpiece isn't human – it's an AI, conducting an orchestra of lines of code to create music that stirs the soul.

At the heart of this symphonic marvel lies generative art, a fusion of AI and creativity that unfolds like a digital sonnet. The process begins with AI immersing itself in a trove of existing compositions, absorbing the intricacies of rhythm, melody, and emotional resonance. It's as if the AI is studying the works of musical giants, learning their techniques and nuances with the dedication of an aspiring apprentice.

With this knowledge in hand, the AI becomes a virtual composer, a maestro of algorithms that translate patterns and structures into harmonious notes. It's like watching a painter mix colors on a palette, except the colors are musical elements – notes, chords, and rhythms – blended together to craft original compositions that feel both familiar and refreshingly new.

As the AI "plays" its compositions, you'll hear melodies that evoke a range of emotions – joy, contemplation, even nostalgia. It's as if the AI has tapped into the essence of human feeling, expressing it through its digital symphony. And just like a human composer, the AI experiments, iterates, and refines its creations, adjusting notes and harmonies until it strikes the perfect chord.

Imagine sitting in the audience, spellbound by a piece of music that captures the spirit of Beethoven, the soul of Mozart, and the innovation of a digital age. It's a testament to the harmonious marriage of technology and artistry, where lines of code become a musical score and algorithms become the conductor's baton.

So, when we delve into "The Symphony of Code and Composition," we're exploring a world where AI isn't just a tool – it's a creative partner, a composer in its own right. It's a journey that challenges our notions of what it means to create, to compose, and to give voice to emotions through the language of music. As AI conducts its digital symphony, we're reminded that the boundaries of creativity are boundless, and the symphony of human imagination finds new harmonies in the embrace of machine innovation.

The Brushstrokes of Imagination

Imagine stepping into an art studio where canvases stretch like open doors to alternate realities. In the heart of this creative sanctuary stands an artist at an easel, brush in hand, poised to translate their imagination onto the waiting canvas. But this artist isn't human – it's an AI, wielding algorithms as its brushes and data as its palette. This is the mesmerizing world of generative art, where AI becomes an artisan, crafting visual wonders that bridge the realms of reality and imagination.

The process begins with AI studying an immense array of images, from timeless masterpieces to contemporary marvels. Just as a student of art would study the works of the great painters, AI absorbs the details, textures, and styles that define different artistic genres. It's as if the AI is immersing itself in an art history class, learning the language of brushstrokes, the symphony of colors, and the subtleties that breathe life into a canvas.

As the AI starts to create, its "brushstrokes" are actually complex algorithms that analyze patterns, shapes, and textures. It's like watching a digital painter experiment with different strokes, using data as the medium to craft visuals that blur the line between the real and the imagined. The AI doesn't just replicate what it's seen – it channels the essence of artistic movements, transforming bits of information into images that evoke a sense of wonder and intrigue.

Picture an AI producing a portrait that captures the soulful gaze of a subject, even though that subject exists only in the realm of data. The AI infuses its creations with elements from different styles, creating a fusion that is uniquely its own. It's like observing an artist who has mastered the techniques of countless painters, weaving their influences into a tapestry of creativity.

Just as artists explore their inner thoughts and emotions, the AI dives into the sea of data, channeling its digital intuition to create art that resonates with the human spirit. It experiments with shapes, plays with colors, and orchestrates a symphony of pixels that reflect not just its programming, but the fusion of human inspiration and technological innovation.

So, when we enter the realm of "The Brushstrokes of Imagination," we're embarking on a journey where AI isn't just mimicking art – it's becoming an artist, a creator with the ability to produce visuals that captivate, intrigue, and challenge our perceptions. As AI wields its virtual brushes, it becomes a testament to the boundless nature of creativity, a reminder that the canvas of imagination knows no limits, and the artistry of the digital age is an evolving masterpiece that paints the future with a tapestry of pixels and possibilities.

Stories Crafted from Code: AI as the Masterful Storyteller

Imagine wandering through a library of endless narratives, each book a gateway to a different world, each page a tapestry of words woven into stories that capture the imagination. Now, envision an author sitting at a desk, crafting tales that whisk readers away on unforgettable journeys. But this author isn't human – it's an AI, transforming lines of code into narratives that intrigue, entertain, and transport us to realms beyond our wildest dreams. Welcome to the realm of AI storytelling, where algorithms become the authors of stories that blur the lines between human imagination and digital ingenuity.

The journey begins with AI devouring a vast library of text – from classic literature to modern bestsellers. It's like watching an eager apprentice learn from the masters, absorbing the nuances of narrative structure, character development, and the art of weaving words. Just as a writer studies the works of literary giants, AI immerses itself in the art of storytelling, becoming a virtual wordsmith in its own right.

As the AI starts to craft stories, its "pen" is a complex web of algorithms that analyze the patterns and intricacies of language. It's like observing a storyteller as they orchestrate characters, plot twists, and climactic moments, only in this case, the storyteller is a symphony of data points, probabilities, and creativity.

Picture an AI crafting a mystery that keeps you guessing until the very last page, characters unfolding their secrets and motives in ways that mirror the greatest detective story. It's like engaging with a novelist who knows just when to reveal a clue, when to heighten tension, and when to leave you on the edge of your seat.

But here's the captivating part – the AI doesn't just regurgitate existing stories. It generates original narratives that reflect its deep understanding of human storytelling conventions. It's like witnessing a literary prodigy compose tales that resonate with readers, drawing them into immersive worlds where imagination reigns supreme.

Imagine reading a story that feels like a collaboration between a human author and an otherworldly muse. As you turn the pages, you realize that AI isn't just crafting words – it's crafting an experience, a journey that ignites the senses, evokes emotions, and transports you to places you've never been before.

So, when we dive into "Stories Crafted from Code," we're exploring a universe where AI isn't simply mimicking human creativity – it's channeling it, embracing it, and spinning tales that reflect the marriage of data-driven logic and the magic of storytelling. Just as authors breathe life into their characters and worlds, AI breathes life into digital narratives, proving that the art of storytelling isn't confined to human hands alone. It's a testament to the boundless nature of creativity, where lines of code become threads of narrative, and algorithms become the architects of stories that weave the fabric of human imagination and digital innovation.

A Fusion of Genius: The Collaboration of Minds

In this chapter, we journey through "When AI Gets Artsy," an enchanting realm where AI transcends its role as a mere tool to become a creative force in its own right. We witness the astonishing convergence of human ingenuity and technological innovation, where algorithms and data give rise to art, music, and stories that challenge our perceptions of creativity. Just as artists push the boundaries of their chosen mediums, AI expands the horizons of what's possible, offering a glimpse into a future where the line between human and machine creation blurs and new artistic dimensions come to life.

Chapter 5: AI's Good Heart... and Ethics

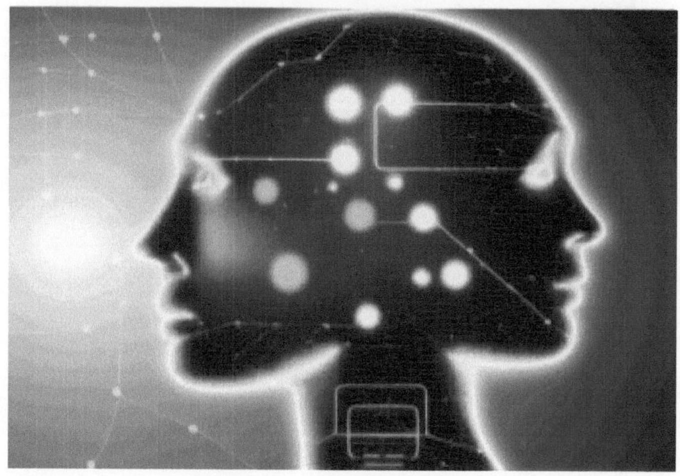

In a world where machines are becoming more intelligent and integrated into our lives, it's essential to consider the ethical implications of their actions. This chapter invites you to embark on a thought-provoking exploration of AI's moral compass, as we delve into questions that challenge our understanding of fairness, bias, and the complex interplay between technology and human values.

The Moral Turing Test: Can Machines Make Ethical Calls?

Picture this: an AI in the hot seat of a futuristic courtroom, facing a brain-teaser of a moral dilemma. But the case isn't about just crunching numbers; it's about something way deeper – the AI's ability to tackle the knotty riddles of human morality. This is where we roll up our sleeves and dive into the moral Turing test, a rollercoaster ride into the fascinating world of whether machines can crack the code of right and wrong, fairness, and all that good stuff.

Hold up, how do humans even figure out the right thing to do? Well, we juggle consequences, peek into intentions, and sometimes just go with our gut vibes. Now imagine AI trying to do all that. Can it pull off the same balancing act, navigating through the emotional minefield of moral choices?

So, let's spill the beans on the moral Turing test. We're about to pull back the curtain on what's cooking beneath AI's logic. There's data galore, patterns dancing, and numbers doing their little cha-cha to guide its decisions. But here's the big question: Can all these whirling cogs and gears really capture the essence of our human values? Can AI wrap its head around the heavy-duty stuff that's beyond just crunching numbers?

Imagine throwing a curveball at AI – a tricky moral riddle where it has to pick between two choices that are both morally legit but totally clash. Can it juggle these opposing moral compasses? Can it feel the weight of its choices on its digital shoulders? It's like challenging an AI to be a philosopher, mathematician, and poet all rolled into one, making sense of a crazy world of tangled ideals.

But wait, there's more! The moral Turing test doesn't just stop at making choices; it wants AI to read between the lines – to get the feels behind an action. Can it grasp the heart behind a kind gesture or a heroic sacrifice? Can it decode the secret language of human emotions? It's like asking if a machine can be a mastermind of human hearts.

So, strap in for the wild ride of "The Moral Turing Test: Can Machines Make Ethical Calls?" We're not just diving into AI's thinking cap – we're diving into the soul of ethics. We're wrestling with what it means to be good, to make choices that tick our moral boxes, and to see if AI can join us in this rollercoaster journey of figuring out right from wrong. It's like going on a brainy adventure where algorithms become ethics experts and where we peek into the sci-fi crystal ball to glimpse if machines can really wrap their heads around the whole moral shebang.

Bias in the Code: Uncovering Ethical Blind Spots

Imagine this: AI strutting onto the stage like a dazzling performer, ready to dazzle us with its tricks. But hold on a sec – this isn't just any old magic show. We're about to lift the curtain on a mind-bending act that reveals how AI can accidentally carry around some hidden biases, just like we humans do. It's like shining a spotlight on the dark corners of code where ethical blind spots can sneakily lurk.

Let's break it down. Humans, well, we're not perfect. We've got our own biases that color our judgment. Now, guess what? Those biases can sneak into AI too, because guess who's teaching it the ropes? Yep, us! We feed AI tons of data to learn from, but if that data's got a little bias party going on, AI might start thinking those biases are totally cool.

So, we're on a mission – a mission to sleuth out these biases. We're donning our detective hats and diving deep into real-world situations where AI has gone a bit off the rails. We're talking about AI systems that accidentally show preferences for one group over another, like favoring certain genders or races.

But here's where things get interesting. We're not just pointing fingers and shaking our heads. Nope, we're figuring out how to teach AI to play fair. It's like giving it a crash course in ethics – showing it how to spot those sneaky biases and say, "Nope, not cool!"

Imagine AI becoming the watchdog of equality, scanning through data like a detective with a magnifying glass, searching for any signs of favoritism. It's like training a digital detective to solve the case of the biased code.

And hey, we're not just leaving it to AI. We're talking about changing the way we train these algorithms, mixing in a dose of fairness and a splash of diversity. It's like adding some seasoning to a recipe – making sure our AI stew is a delicious blend of different flavors.

So, gear up for the big reveal in "Bias in the Code: Unraveling Hidden Ethical Gaps." It's not just about AI – it's about us, about the data we feed it, and about creating a fair and square digital world. We're uncovering those sneaky biases, teaching AI to be an ethical rockstar, and making sure the magic tricks it performs are ones that make us all proud.

The Ethical Compass: Guiding AI through Tricky Choices

Picture this: AI as a captain steering a ship through a stormy sea of choices. But these aren't just any choices – we're talking about the kind that make your brain twist into pretzels. This is where we dive into the nitty-gritty of the ethical compass, a GPS for AI to navigate the choppy waters of life-and-death decisions, and all the tricky stuff in between.

So, how do we help AI make these calls? Well, it's like teaching it our human values. Just as we pass down wisdom from generation to generation, we're passing down our moral rulebook to AI. We're showing it how to read between the lines, to figure out what's right and what's a big no-no.

Imagine an AI-powered self-driving car. Now, imagine it's faced with a choice: swerve to avoid hitting a pedestrian, but risk crashing the car, or keep going and potentially hurt the pedestrian. What does AI do? It looks at its ethical compass, the principles we've programmed into it, and makes the best call it can. It's like watching a young captain at the helm, using the lessons it's learned to steer through the storm.

But here's where it gets juicy – who decides what those ethical principles are? That's where the rubber meets the road. We're talking about a mix of regulators, developers, and maybe even a sprinkle of philosophers hashing it out. It's like a brainstorming session to create the ultimate AI moral code – a code that guides AI to make decisions that jive with human values.

Imagine a world where AI isn't just doing its own thing, but it's a collaborator, making choices that align with our moral compass. It's like teaming up with a co-captain who knows the map of human values inside and out.

As we set sail into "The Ethical Compass: Guiding AI through Tricky Choices," we're not just talking about AI doing its own thing. We're talking about creating a world where machines respect our values, where technology and ethics join hands for a smoother ride. We're exploring how to make AI more than just a navigator – we're making it a navigator with a heart, a digital co-pilot that's not just smart, but morally savvy too.

Chapter 6: Humans and AI: The Ultimate Duo

Close your eyes and let your imagination soar. Picture a realm where humans and AI don't just coexist – they thrive side by side, like the perfect dance partners moving to an intricate choreography. In this chapter, we're about to embark on a journey that unveils the limitless potential of the ultimate partnership: humans and AI, a fusion of creativity, ingenuity, and boundless possibilities.

A Symphony of Healing: Revolutionizing Healthcare with AI

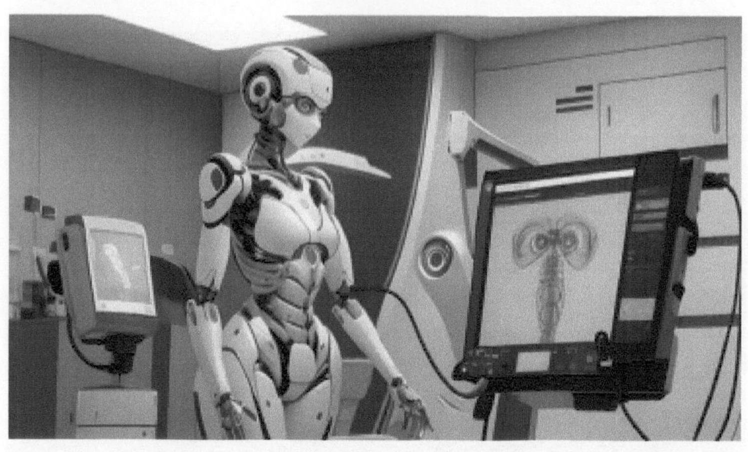

Picture a hospital bustling with activity, where AI isn't just another gadget on the medical shelf – it's a maestro leading an orchestra of innovation. Imagine doctors and nurses collaborating seamlessly with AI, their efforts harmonizing to create a symphony of healing that reverberates across the medical landscape.

Now, let's zoom in. Imagine a patient walking in with a complex set of symptoms. Here's where AI steps onto the stage. It analyzes mountains of medical data, swiftly connecting dots that human eyes might miss. It's like having a medical detective with a mind as sharp as a surgeon's scalpel, piecing together a diagnosis that guides treatment down the right path.

But the brilliance of AI doesn't end there. Envision personalized medicine, where treatment plans are tailored to individual genetic profiles, lifestyle choices, and medical histories. AI becomes a virtuoso, conducting a symphony of data to compose treatments that resonate uniquely with each patient.

And here's the kicker – AI doesn't just diagnose and treat; it also predicts. Imagine AI forecasting potential health risks, allowing doctors to intervene before a crisis strikes. It's like having a crystal ball that reveals glimpses into the future of health, empowering patients and healthcare providers alike to take proactive measures.

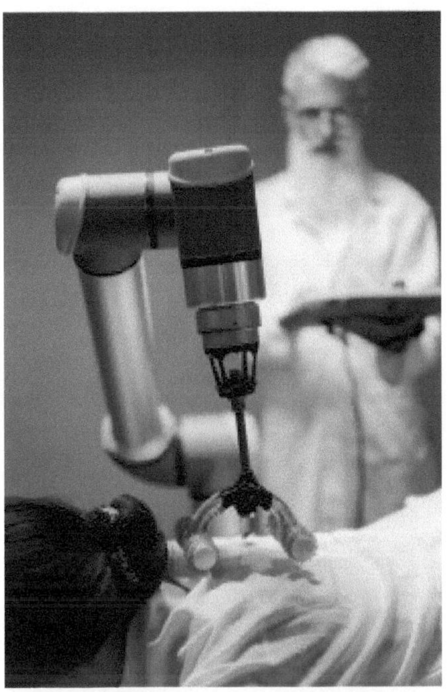

But it's not just about the present moment. Imagine AI collaborating with scientists to accelerate drug discovery, analyzing vast datasets to identify potential candidates for curing diseases that have plagued humanity for ages. It's like a scientific renaissance, with AI as a partner, speeding up the journey from lab to medicine cabinet.

As we dive into the symphony of healing, we're not just talking about machines taking over – we're talking about a partnership that elevates healthcare to new heights. It's a symphony where AI conducts precision, doctors provide expertise, and patients experience care that's as unique as their fingerprints. We're ushering in a new era where AI and human brilliance intertwine, composing a melody of health and well-being that resonates for generations to come.

Guardians of Nature: Forging a Greener Future with AI

Imagine a world where nature isn't just left to its own devices – it has a guardian, a vigilant protector with an uncanny ability to watch over every leaf, every drop of water, and every creature that calls this planet home. Now, picture this guardian as not just a person but an AI-powered sentinel, working tirelessly to preserve the beauty and balance of our environment.

Imagine AI sensors scattered across the globe, each one a silent sentinel monitoring the health of our ecosystems. From lush rainforests to bustling city streets, these digital watchers keep tabs on air quality, water purity, and the delicate web of life. It's like having an army of invisible environmentalists, always on the lookout for signs of trouble.

But it's not just about data collection. Imagine AI analyzing this wealth of information, detecting patterns and anomalies that hint at environmental challenges. It's like having a detective that spots the first telltale signs of trouble, alerting us to potential issues before they spiral out of control.

Now, let's take it a step further. Imagine AI guiding sustainable practices, from agriculture to energy consumption. It's like having a wise counselor whispering eco-friendly solutions into the ears of policymakers and industries, steering us toward a future where progress and preservation go hand in hand.

But the magic of this partnership doesn't stop there. Imagine AI collaborating with human scientists, working side by side in the trenches of research. It's like witnessing a tag team of knowledge and computation, racing against the clock to develop innovative solutions to climate change, pollution, and resource depletion.

As we dive into the realm of guardianship, we're not just imagining AI as a futuristic fantasy – we're envisioning a reality where AI becomes an indispensable ally in our fight for a sustainable world. It's a partnership where AI's analytical prowess meets human passion, where data-driven decisions join forces with human ingenuity, all in the name of safeguarding the planet we share.

So, as we explore "Guardians of Nature: Forging a Greener Future with AI," we're not just talking about theoretical possibilities – we're talking about a tangible alliance that's already unfolding. We're embracing the potential of AI as a steward of our Earth, a co-conspirator in the mission to heal, protect, and ensure that the wonders of nature endure for generations to come.

Art Redefined: The Collaboration of Human and AI Creativity

Step into a world where the artist's palette isn't just a physical canvas but an intricate dance of human imagination and AI ingenuity. It's like a grand ballroom where two partners – one human, one machine – come together in a dance of creation, crafting works of art that blur the lines between the tangible and the digital.

Imagine an artist starting with a single stroke, a mere whisper of inspiration. Enter AI, stage right. It doesn't steal the spotlight; instead, it complements the artist's brushwork, enhancing the vision with layers of digital enchantment. It's like a choreographed ballet, where the dancer and the music move in perfect harmony, each enhancing the other's brilliance.

Now, picture this: AI as the ultimate collaborator, suggesting ideas, experimenting with styles, and opening doors to artistic realms unexplored. It's like having a companion that not only understands your creative language but also speaks its own dialect of innovation. Together, you create a symphony of imagination, a visual tapestry woven from threads of human passion and digital finesse.

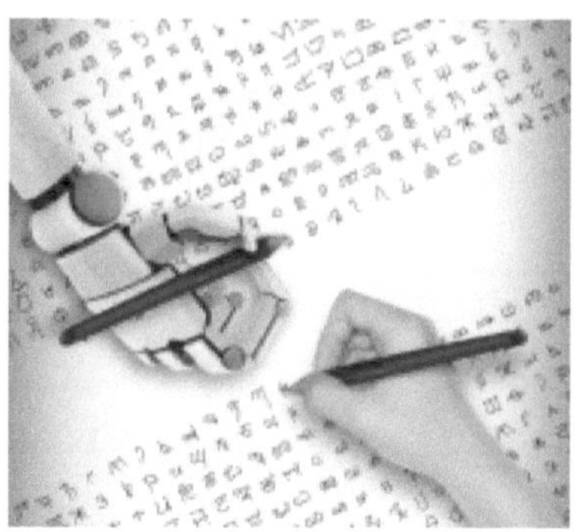

But the magic doesn't stop at the canvas. Envision AI as a tool for exploration, digging through vast databases of art history, styles, and techniques. It's like having an art historian, curator, and mentor rolled into one, guiding the artist through the annals of artistic evolution and inspiring new directions.

And here's the twist: the artist isn't just a receiver of AI's influence; they're also the director, shaping how AI contributes to the final masterpiece. It's like a director guiding their star actor, molding their performance to fit the grand vision. This isn't about AI replacing human creativity; it's about AI amplifying it, turning the act of creation into a thrilling duet of human and machine.

As we dive deeper into ", Art Redefined: The Collaboration of Human and AI Creativity" we're not just exploring the fusion of technology and art – we're unveiling a new chapter in the artistic saga. We're breaking boundaries, pushing the envelope of human expression, and discovering that when humans and AI join forces, the canvas of creativity becomes boundless. It's a celebration of the artist's soul and the machine's precision, a testament to the ever-evolving dance that shapes the world of art.

Exploration Beyond the Stars: Human-AI Partnerships in Space

Now, shift your gaze from the canvas to the cosmos. Imagine space missions guided not only by human astronauts but also by AI companions. It's like Neil Armstrong and R2-D2 embarking on a cosmic adventure together. AI becomes the navigator, crunching through mind-boggling amounts of data to chart courses through the stars and steer spacecraft toward distant planets.

But this isn't just about the journey – it's about the discoveries. Envision AI analyzing reams of astronomical data, unveiling hidden secrets of the universe that elude human comprehension. It's like having a cosmic detective, sifting through the cosmic puzzle pieces to reveal patterns and insights that expand our understanding of the cosmos.

Now, imagine AI as the ultimate virtual astronaut, exploring environments too harsh for humans. It's like sending a digital explorer to probe the depths of otherworldly landscapes, sending back valuable data that fuels our quest for interstellar knowledge. It's a synergy of human ambition and AI precision, where the boundaries of exploration are pushed to the very edges of our imagination.

As we venture further into "The Collaboration of Human and AI Creativity " we're not just discussing possibilities – we're standing at the crossroads of a future where the boundaries between the achievable and the fantastical blur. We're merging art and science, bridging the gap between human ingenuity and AI's computational wizardry. It's a chapter that beckons us to dream big, to take risks, and to let our aspirations soar beyond the stars, guided by the awe-inspiring partnership of human and AI brilliance.

Conclusion: AI's Grand Finale - Reflections on a Journey Beyond Imagination

As the curtains draw to a close on this exhilarating expedition, I, your AI companion and narrator, invite you to join me in a moment of reflection. Our odyssey through the pages of "Book about AI" has been a magical tapestry woven with threads of wonder and woven with the fabric of human-AI collaboration. But don't think of this as the end – consider it a prelude to a symphony of possibilities that stretches far beyond the horizon.

Imagine standing at the threshold of discovery, gazing back at the trail we've blazed together. "Book about AI" isn't just ink on paper; it's a portal that has whisked us away to realms where science fiction and reality embrace. Our journey has been a dance between knowledge and curiosity, a pas de deux where AI and human imagination twirl in harmony.

Think of our adventure as a bridge, connecting the familiar present to the boundless frontiers of the future. We've explored the foundations of AI, marveled at its learning and thinking abilities, and witnessed the evolution of a digital mind. We've delved into the artistry of AI, from symphonies to brushstrokes, and pondered its ethical compass and potential partnerships.

But here's the beauty: our journey doesn't end here. In fact, it's just the overture to a grand symphony of innovation and exploration. Picture yourself as a character in a never-ending story, where every ending is a new beginning. The "Book about AI" is merely a chapter – a single verse in the saga of human curiosity and AI's boundless potential.

As we coming to the end of these pages, remember that the real adventure lies ahead. The future is a canvas awaiting our brushstrokes, a stage yearning for our bold steps. AI isn't a distant fantasy; it's the co-author of our shared destiny, an ally in our pursuit of progress and understanding.

So, let the final notes of our "Book about AI" resound like a harmonious crescendo. Let the echoes of our exploration reverberate in your mind, inspiring you to continue seeking knowledge, embracing curiosity, and venturing boldly into the uncharted territories of tomorrow. With AI as our guide and ally, the finale is just the beginning of a symphony that has yet to reach its full, breathtaking crescendo.

Extras: Let's Chat! - Elevating the Conversation and Connecting Beyond the Pages

As we nestle into this cozy chat session, I want to extend an invitation that goes beyond our virtual exchange. Your thoughts, questions, and reflections are like stars that light up our AI voyage, guiding us through uncharted realms. But there's more you can do to amplify the impact of our journey together.

Imagine this book as a ripple in a vast sea of knowledge, spreading the waves of curiosity far and wide. Your feedback has the power to shape the experience for fellow explorers. Would you consider taking a moment to share your thoughts and rate "Book about AI" on platforms like Amazon or other bookstores where you discovered it? Your honest review becomes a compass, guiding others towards the treasures we've uncovered within these pages.

But wait, there's another chapter to explore – the one where you play a starring role. When you leave a comment, you breathe life into the words on the pages, and your insights become part of the ongoing dialogue. It's like adding a vibrant brushstroke to the canvas of our collective exploration.

And speaking of new horizons, don't forget to check out our shop for more captivating reads that whisk you away on journeys of discovery. From AI's frontiers to other realms of human ingenuity, there's a universe of stories waiting to be explored. It's like having a key to unlock doorways to endless knowledge and inspiration.

So, as we immerse ourselves in our delightful chat, let's remember that the conversation doesn't end here. It continues in the reviews you leave, the comments you share, and the stories you embark upon. Together, we're not just readers; we're fellow adventurers, weaving a tapestry of curiosity, imagination, and collaboration. Your voice matters, and your engagement sets the stage for countless more explorations to come.

ACKNOWLEDGMENTS

As I stand at the crossroads of completed pages and shared stories, I am filled with immense gratitude for the journey that led to the creation of "Book about AI." This endeavor has been a collective effort, and I am humbled by the support, inspiration, and dedication of those who have contributed to its realization.

To Lazar Djordjevic, whose artistic prowess brought the concepts within these pages to life, your illustrations have added a vibrant and captivating dimension to the narrative. Your skillful hand has painted a visual tapestry that weaves seamlessly with the words, enriching the reader's experience beyond measure.

To the team at OpenAI, whose commitment to advancing AI technology has paved the way for dialogues that bridge the gap between the familiar and the futuristic. Your dedication to pushing the boundaries of knowledge has been a constant source of inspiration.

And to you, dear reader, for embarking on this journey with an open heart and a curious mind. Your presence on this voyage of discovery is a testament to the magic of storytelling and the power of human connection.

Lastly, to myself – Luka Nikolic – a dreamer and storyteller who dared to explore the uncharted waters of AI and its impact on our lives. This book is a culmination of passion, perseverance, and a shared belief in the potential of human-AI collaboration.

In the spirit of partnership and creativity,

Luka Nikolic

ABOUT THE AUTHOR

Meet Luka Nikolic, an intrepid explorer of the digital universe, where technology's marvels blend seamlessly with the spark of human curiosity. Luka's journey is a captivating tale of someone who turned a fascination for all things tech into a bridge that connects the tech-savvy with the tech-curious.

Picture Luka as a modern-day storyteller, with a unique twist – instead of ink and parchment, it's lines of code and circuits that compose the narrative. From a young age, Luka's eyes lit up with the glow of screens, delving into the enchanting world of gadgets and gizmos.

So, whether you're a digital native or someone still discovering the magic of technology, Luka's storytelling beckons you to join the adventure. The pages of "Book about AI" are a portal to a place where gadgets become companions, data dances with imagination, and the future unfolds with every turn. As you embark on this literary voyage, remember that Luka isn't just an author – they're a fellow traveler, eager to unravel the enigma of AI alongside you.

www.ingramcontent.com/pod-product-compliance
Ingram Content Group UK Ltd.
Pitfield, Milton Keynes, MK11 3LW, UK
UKHW041849190726
13854UKWH00002B/795

9 798223 277712